John A. Reaves

WILL

I

ALWAYS BE

BE A ███

IN AMERICA?

A Black Man's Reflections on Living in America

Printed in the United States of America

Print ISBN: 978-1-7357030-0-8
E-Book ISBN: 978-1-7357030-1-5

**Canoe Tree
Press**

4697 Main Street
Manchester Center, VT 05255
Canoe Tree Press is a division of DartFrog Books.

CONTENTS

 WILL I ALWAYS BE A ▓▓▓▓▓ IN AMERICA

INTRODUCTION

I believe in America where everyone's life matters and no one will ever be left behind. I believe in an America that puts out its hand to pull you up when you're down and gives you as many chances as you need to stand. I believe in an America where hate is replaced by love and hope is restored from despair. I do believe that better days are ahead of us, but as a Black man, the only country I have lived in and known makes me and others that look like me feel as if our lives do not matter. Regardless of what I contribute to this country, I will always be seen and treated as a Black man. When typing Black in Google's search engine, the following definition appears: *any human group having dark-colored skin, especially of African or Australian Aboriginal ancestry.* I'm glad the definition recognizes Black people

as human, for there was a time we were not recognized as such. Nevertheless, we are so much more than this definition, and our skin should not define us or anyone else who is not white.

I was prompted to write *Will I Always Be A*  *In America* −10 essays that I wrote to share my feelings and experience as a Black man in America. Being an educated Black man with several academic and professional accomplishments, my sense of being is reduced to my skin color.

As the title asks, how do you view Black men in America? If the answer to this question cannot be shared in a public forum, then you must ask yourself why you cannot share your answer and what, if anything, can be done to change your answer? I hope the spirit of my essays that highlights a small representation of my experiences as a young boy, teenager, and adult will resonate with some, spark discussion with others, and most importantly, encourage others to see Black men for what we are, *Men*.

We are in a season where race has dominated our airwaves and many people are expressing their fatigue of hearing and discussing this subject. It is my belief that as long as there is institutional racism that impedes people of color—especially Black men—from living the promise of life wherever they choose to live in America, the discussions must continue. Our societal reality is that race has been a discussion since the creation of the United States on July 4, 1776. The discussion has taken many twists and turns, and there has been some improvements since the initial discussion. The question is — do we ever plan to find solutions to put these discussions to an end, or will Black men like myself and other people of color continue to ask, "Will I always be a ████ in America" beyond 2020?

—John A. Reaves

Matthews, North Carolina

August 31, 2020

We cannot control who and what we see, but we can control "...how we respond" once we see them.

ACKNOWLEDGMENTS

I am so fortunate to have a support system that aspires me to be whatever I want to be and live my life as I choose to live it. I am so grateful for my loving spouse, Denise who continuously provides the right blend of love, respect and support when needed; My kids, Francis, Kayla and Micah who have been my rock and provides me with fuel to be the best version of myself. My mother, Frances Reaves and sisters – Debra, Renee and Sandra who all provided me with encouragement in their own way. My in-laws, Ray and Lois Goodall for their unconditional support and to my close friends Edmund Fleet and Denice Bond who I consider family members and part of my extended support system. My thanks also to WordWiz for helping me with edits and making helpful suggestions.

WE WANT TO LIVE

June 1, 1977 is a date that I will never forget—for it is the day my world shattered. Early that morning, I heard my father, William Roger Reaves, in the bathroom; when he came out, I shot out of bed to tell him good-bye as he prepared to go to work. A few hours later, the phone rang moments before I left for school, and when I said "Hello," the caller asked whether there was an adult at home. I said "No," and she indicated that someone needed to get to Loudon Hospital as soon as possible. She asked me to write down the phone number, and I did.

I had no idea what she was talking about, so I called my sister, who was a teacher at a middle school across the street from our apartment building, and she rushed over and called the number. As my sister was speaking, my mom walked in the door

from her nursing assistant's job and heard her on the phone with the hospital. She told my mom immediately that my dad was ill and they both ran out of the door to drive to the hospital, which was an hour from our home. Unfortunately, by the time they arrived, it was too late, as my dad had died already from a massive heart attack. When my mom and sister returned home, I knew what had happened instantly because my mother was sobbing silently. Not knowing what to do or how to console her, I went to my room and stared out of the window, thinking that it was just a dream and that my father would walk through the door after his shift ended.

His death came without any warnings or final good-byes. I wondered if my father's skin color was a factor in the care he received when he was taken to the hospital before his death. I have wondered what my life would have been like had my father been alive to share some critical milestones in my life: my high school and college graduations; the purchase of my first car and home; my wedding; the births of my children: and celebrating my first Father's Day. While I will never experience these significant events with my father, I am grateful to be alive to celebrate numerous achievements with my spouse and children.

Generally, on June 1, I recognize my father's passing by saying a prayer and then calling my niece to wish her a happy birthday. This year was quite different, not only because of the approximately 200,000+ deaths related to COVID-19, but also the heinous murders of Breonna Taylor, Ahmaud Arbery, George Floyd, and Rayshard Brooks. What all of these terrible deaths have in common with my father's death is that there were no final good-byes. Each of them left behind a multitude of family and friends who loved them unconditionally, with no regard for what they had accomplished in life or their skin color.

I thought COVID-19 would unite us as a nation because of how it randomly afflicts those who are healthy or those with preexisting illnesses. I thought COVID-19 would bring us together because so many of us can empathize with the death of someone we love.

I felt that death was an equalizer for humanity, but even with death, some people still believe people of color, particularly Black men, are not worthy of living. To those who think this, I say *we want to live!*

We want to live a life where we can breathe air, watch the sun rise, and daydream about the possibilities of true freedom where the only qualification required is human existence. We want to live in a country where all lives are meaningful; if death falls on our doorstep, it is only because of natural causes.

We want to live in a world where a Black man can jog in any neighborhood or stand in an elevator and hold his head high without someone calling the police, clutching their purse, or wondering if he will be harmed simply because of that person's skin color.

As Black men, we want to go to the hospital and receive high-quality care without the presumption that all Black men are supermen and do not require medication to fight ailments. We want to live in a society where a Black man can ask questions or engage in discourse without being killed. I know this is the twenty-first century—and it is hard to believe many people in our society do not welcome such requests—but people of color should not have to plead to live.

Let us honor the tens of thousands of people of color who lost their lives because of their skin color by individually looking in the mirror and asking ourselves, "Do Black lives matter?" Our verbal answer to this question matters, but our actions when no one is looking will matter more.

WILL THE PEOPLE FINALLY END RACISM IN AMERICA?

The United States is fighting a raging pandemic, tackling a recession, and circumnavigating through racial injustice. Many of us ushered in 2020 with the hopes of good health and prosperity but had no idea that the events of 2020 would attack our bodies, minds, and wallets. For people of color, injustice lives in the fringes of our psyches. Today, it has rightfully catapulted to the ranks but not above COVID-19 and the recession. All are holding our country hostage, and we are desperate for swift solutions. The pandemic and recession are likely to be contained soon but this is less likely for racial justice.

In most major cities in the United States, millions of people from all walks of life are protesting

the racial inequalities that have subjugated our country since August 20, 1619. This date marked the birth of slavery in the United States. The National Archives, the government entity that preserves all US records, deems these three documents, the Declaration of Independence (1776), the US Constitution (1787), and the Bills of Rights (1791), collectively as the Charters of Freedom.[1]

Each of these documents contributed to forming the governance of the United States. Two hundred forty-four years later, legislation, in theory, was supposed to eliminate racial injustice and supremacy. It instead institutionalized it, and from the surface, it appears by design. By no surprise, all the persons who created these documents had no vested interest in enacting equitable freedom for Black, brown, women, or any other type of person who did not look like them or share their wealth.

From the 1863 Emancipation Proclamation to the 1964 Civil Rights Act, several laws and measures, such as Quotas and Affirmative Action, have been formed to govern racial discrimination. Regrettably, none of these initiatives have eliminated it. The question becomes: can we end racial injustice in the United States?

The quick answer is yes, but what will it take to deinstitutionalize 401 years of racism? Do we need a commission on racial justice to discuss this issue for another four hundred years? What about new legislation that offers a way for our country to move forward without rewarding the systems that manufactured racism in the first place? What about reparations? What about a payment system to financially make all people of color whole? The idea of reparations comes with questions of its own: why would any non-person of color vote for such an approach to solving racial injustice? Who would pay for it, and who would receive it?

In other words, there are no easy answers to addressing this problem. A step forward would be for "We the People of the United States" to first stop disputing that racial inequity plagues our country. Too many centuries have been spent arguing and debating this fact. It would be great for the United States to provide an example to the civilized world of how to solve this problem that has plagued our country for over four hundred years, but first things first. We need to admit and own our problem. No real progress can occur on racial injustice in the US until this action occurs at the highest level of our government.

What I appreciate about the United States is our ingenuity and the beacon of hope that resonates with most people worldwide. We are a great country, and I have no desire to live in any other country.

An opportunity for "We the People of the United States" is to finally make our country *great* by no longer being the dictionary definition for racial injustice. Inspirational words and softball legislation have fueled this inequity for way too long.

What is frustrating about the United States is our failure to act. Why is it taking so long to eliminate racism? Do we really like being a laughingstock among nations? Sadly, the problem of racism is not confined to the United States, and most countries struggle with this issue. I suppose what makes the struggle in the United States a little different than what other countries are experiencing is the last lines of the inscription on the Statue of Liberty, also known as the New Colossus, written by Emma Lazarus that reads

> *"Give me your tired, your poor,*
> *Your huddled masses yearning to breathe free,*
> *The wretched refuse of your teeming shore.*
> *Send these, the homeless, tempest-tossed to me,*
> *I lift my lamp beside the golden door!"*

In other words, it professes to be a country that was built on a sea of ethnicities and races and everyone is equal. I believe we got the building part right but enjoying what was built and the equity piece is where the problem lies.

As a country, we must again admit we have a problem, address it, and take responsibility for our previous inaction. We must be willing as individuals to call out all instances of racial injustice in our homes, in our communities, in our jobs, in our schools, in our churches, in our governments—in all places where this ugly cancer exists. As a society, we must eliminate the institutional walls of silent racism by requiring everyone to pay a tax on reforming the system. We must reject polite racism by voting for elected officials whose actions complement their words. We must raise our hands when we are in positions of influence and wealth and stop asking why people of color are not at the table and instead bring them to the table. "We the People" can make all these things possible, but it is the "Will of the People" that can finally eliminate racial injustice.

THE NEIGHBORHOODS I LIVE AND RUN THROUGH: ARE THEY A SYMBOL OF OPTIMISM OR A DEATH TRAP?

Not long ago, I glanced out of the window, and two persons with flowers approached my front door. Father's Day had come and gone, so I knew it was not a belated Father's Day gift. I had not ordered any flowers for my spouse, at least not this week. Once I heard a knock at the door, I opened it, and the persons identified themselves as my neighbors. In the advent of COVID, I appreciated they stayed six feet away from my door and wore masks. They placed a beautiful bouquet of wildflowers from their garden on my doorstep and said they wanted to say hello and wanted to get to know the neighbors. After exchanging a few pleasantries, we said good-bye, and they were on their way.

I'm not sure if these neighbors had seen me running through the neighborhood or not. Whatever the case, I appreciated their kind gesture and hope it motivates other neighbors to do the same. This act of kindness is also an excellent metaphor for me to keep in mind as I run through my neighborhood. As a Black man, you never know who is watching you or what is going through people's minds as you make your way past their house or street.

Many of us have heard of a booby trap—a device designed to surprise, maim, or kill a person or animal. Sometimes, these devices are intentionally laced with bait to attract its target. The lure for Ahmaud Arbery (a man killed while jogging through a suburban neighborhood while Black) may have been the quiet neighborhood with sidewalks surrounded by freshly cut grass.

I think about Ahmaud Arbery every time I run through my neighborhood. Like Ahmaud, running is an escape for me. I attempt to block out the events of the coming day by imagining a world full of possibilities and hope. As much as I hate to admit it, I never completely blocked out the world as I ran because, as a Black man, I have no idea of what booby trap awaits me as I enter a subdivision or run around a cul-de-sac.

Most of the neighborhoods I run through contain mature trees that line the street, manicured lawns, and non-people of color that generally stare at me as I make my way down the public road. The stares usually soften after they have seen me run past their house a few times. In addition to my visible skin color, I tend to color coordinate my jogging gear from head to toe. This is more of my personal preference, as opposed to dressing for the streets. However, my mind does wonder if my color-coordinated outfits will save me from harassment or possible death. While I may not have the luxury to entirely escape perceptions or possible harm, even in my neighborhood, I do believe there are a few tips that everyone should follow when running or jogging in or outside of your community.

The first drill is to wave at everyone and smile. This may be a little hard when training for a race, but face it, most of us are only running or walking to get in some exercise and fresh air. Next, run on the sidewalk or run in the street in the opposite direction of traffic. Another custom I tend to follow is when approaching a walker or jogger, I make sure I stay to my left or if there is space available, safely run ahead of the walker or jogger and cross back to the left.

I have been running in a variety of neighborhoods for decades. Most of the persons that live or walk

through these neighborhoods do not look like me. From Pennsylvania to Texas, reactions to me when I run through their community for the first time have been the same. First stares, and after a few times of seeing me, I receive smiles and waves.

I would like to believe, if neighborhood-watch personnel sees me running through a neighborhood, they do not chase me down, and when they cannot catch me, retreat to their car, get their gun and shoot at me as if I am a wild animal. I would like to believe if I am confronted by the police, whether my smiles and waves will prompt my neighbors into action and shield me from a life-or-death altercation. I would like to believe running through communities of manicured lawns and tree-lined streets are not only reserved for certain types of persons and dogs.

I believe life should not be this complex for anyone of color, especially for a Black man. There should not be any hidden rules of engagement for a person of color wanting to run or enjoy the tranquility of a neighborhood. Like my neighbors bringing us flowers, there are so many ways to respond to an unfamiliar face in your community. Reaching for your cell phone to call the police is not one of them.

WE HEARD YOU, JOHN ROBERT LEWIS

As human beings, we are all ticking time bombs—not in the sense of carrying explosives, but in possessing a biological clock that will stop when our time on earth is up. Many of us ignore our biological clock with the assumption that money, fame, medicine, and machines will save us, but in the end, when our time is up, our bomb detonates.

On the night of July 17, 2020, an explosion with a significant impact occurred when Legislator John Robert Lewis—a giant in the racial and social justice movement—departed this earth to get some rest finally. He endured over a half-century of physical, mental, and psychological combat that inspired him to push forward in his quest for racial and social justice. If given a choice, he would undoubtedly have chosen to stay in the fight to rebuild a better America.

Now, we must take the arsenal of change that Mr. Lewis spent his life fighting for and apply the following words he so powerfully uttered every time he had the chance: "When you see something that is not right, not fair, not just, you have to speak up, and you have to do something."

I appreciate this statement because it includes all people—black, brown, white, and others—and implores them to stop being silent when confronted with racial injustice. The examples of prejudice are too many and too painful to mention in this commemorative essay for Mr. Lewis. His main point is that we *all* know that if something does not look right, feel right, or sound right, then we must spring into action and get into, as Mr. Lewis would say, "Good Trouble." Each of us must define our interpretation of good trouble as doing nothing and making people of color fight alone do not honor the objective of getting into good trouble.

For me, good trouble is writing about my experiences as a Black man. At times, I feel a little trepidation because I have no idea who will read my essays or how they will be interpreted, or if a violent episode of some kind is in my future. Whatever the case may be, I take solace in the words spoken by Mr. Lewis: "You must be bold, brave, and courageous and find a way ... to get in the way." This pronouncement is a bit terrifying, but John Lewis and many others who dedicated their lives to seeking racial equality have provided more than enough encouragement to turn our fears into actions.

There is hymn titled, "May the Work I've Done Speak for Me." The following is the chorus of that song:

> *The work I've done, it seems so small.*
> *Sometimes it seems like, seems like noth-*
> *ing all.*
> *But when I stand before my God,*
> *I want to hear him say, "Well done."*
> *May the work I've done speak for me.*

When I think about Mr. Lewis and his exceptional accomplishments, it is wonderful knowing that he lived a life that we all should aspire to emulate. His selfless contributions to the human race transcend racial, social, and economic boundaries. There will be no shortage of well-deserved accolades about his life from many people from all walks of life. The question that we all must contemplate as we face our mortality is: Who will speak for us when we depart this life and, most importantly, what will they say?

REIMAGING AMERICA'S EDUCATION SYSTEM: RACE MUST BE A FACTOR

I n 2017, the Pew Research Center, a nonpartisan think tank that informs the public about the issues, attitudes, and trends shaping the world, ranked all industrial countries' student performance in science, mathematics, and reading.[2] The United States did not rank in the top 20 in any of the categories. I can only imagine—with fear—what the 2020 rankings will be because the United States rank probably has slipped since 2017.

Why do I suppose America is ranked so poorly in these rankings? There are numerous contributors. One reality is many Americans do not care about who educates our children and, sadly, how they are educated. Since March 2020, kids around the

nation have received a hodgepodge of learning instruction from their schools, parents, the internet, and, in some cases, the streets. It is so easy to blame COVID-19 for this nightmare, but if we look back at the Pew Research Center results, the wheels have been coming off of the US education infrastructure way before 2020—with no improvement in sight.

As millions of children return to the classroom in person, online, or through a combination of the two, we as a country must finally address what we are going to do to prepare all kids for success. Yes, I believe any kid can learn and succeed—under the right circumstances. Arthur Ashe, a famous tennis player, stated, "Start where you are. Use what you have. Do what you can." In other words, we have an opportunity to reimagine how we educate our kids, and we do not have to wait to start.

Private education has its merits and disadvantages, and due to COVID-19, many more parents (like it or not) have become part of the private education landscape. This unsolicited status may not change in the foreseeable future. Many of us understand public education to be a place that allows most kids access to a classroom but not necessarily an education. Thanks to COVID-19, many parents are experiencing what teachers have faced for decades: performing multiple roles to support our kids—teacher, confidant, disciplinarian, social worker, psychologist, and more. Of course, our private schools' teachers are not exempt from these multiple roles; the main difference is the parents pay tuition for these underlying services.

One of the first things we can all do to reimagine the educational system in the United States is to stop pushing one-size-fits-all approaches to educate our kids. This starts at home. Whether you are a store clerk or CEO of a corporation, take advantage of the time you have with your kids at home to understand their learning styles. It will go a long way. Without getting too technical, some kids respond to visual learning—graphs, charts, symbols—while others learn through listening or auditory learning. An article in Grade Power Learning (gradepowerlearing.com) titled "What Type of Learner Is Your Child?" provides some very helpful tips on determining your child's learning style.[3]

This is important because the education your kid is receiving at their school may not be customized to what they need to succeed. Most teachers do not have the time or bandwidth to access your kid's learning style, and for some kids, this can lead to being placed in remedial education classes because they do not learn the same way as another kid.

Speaking of remedial classes, when our youngest son started his academic journey, we enrolled him at the private school where his sister was enrolled. Unlike his sister, the road was far from smooth. The teacher said our kid was not ready for preschool and needed to repeat. My spouse and I were utterly outraged that his teacher made this suggestion. It was our understanding that preschool was designed to prepare kids for kindergarten. After several conversations, the teacher recommended that we allow the school to test our son to determine if there were any developmental issues and if he was ready to advance to kindergarten. We agreed to the test, and after receiving nearly a perfect score, the teacher still insisted our son was not prepared to advance to kindergarten.

My spouse and I learned early that particularly with young Black boys, the education system as we know it (private or public) tends to misdiagnose Black boys' learning style as a developmental problem. Most of our findings were based on friends and colleagues who have Black or Brown boys and indicated they had similar experiences with their child's teachers and had to barter with the school to keep them out of the remedial classes. It had been our experience that some teachers with little time to properly diagnose Black boys—because of their workload or lack of resources—blanketly recommend them for remedial education classes. An article titled "Black

Minds Matter" written by Tolerance.org highlights this issue that continues to be pervasive in classrooms with Black boys.[4]

For some parents, allowing their kid to repeat a grade may be justifiable because of developmental concerns. Other parents may hold their kid back for strategic reasons, such as to excel in sports or to have the edge over their younger counterparts. We believed our son was ready to move forward, and we did not want him to be held back because of a teacher's misdiagnosis of a learning problem that did not exist. Many Black boys without parents or an advocate who can speak on their behalf end up getting the short end of an increasingly long stick. Their stick tends to result in outcomes that are outside of the scope of this essay.

The racial and economic disparities in our educational system are no secret. Kids in higher social-economic environments have access to more resources, including tutors and tools such as laptops with internet access and accelerated curriculums. Coincidentally, these students with more resources do not measure up to their peers in other countries, which indicates the US educational system appears to be failing all of our students.

Another thing we must do as a country is to rebuild our educational system by investing more money into the system and developing programs that align with all of our society's needs versus the current categories we lump people in, whether in college, military, hospitality, vocational jobs, or prison. All students can learn, but education does not mean all students must go to college. We must give tremendous respect to training programs that teach vocational trades and prepare our non-college bound or military students for careers that will arm them with options to earn a livable wage.

It has been said, "If you are not willing to learn, no one can help you. If you are determined to learn, no one can stop you." I can imagine an educational system in America where all kids are encouraged to dream big, and the learning process can take place inside and outside of the classroom. I can imagine our kids learning to speak and write at least two languages before they reach high school. Where they can master reading in preschool, welcome the wonders of science and technology before entering the first grade, and take algebra before they have reached the fourth grade.

Our legislatures at all levels of the government have the platform to execute all of these grand plans. We have a lifetime to reduce our deficits. We must take this moment to reimagine our educational system by investing in raising the salaries of our teachers to acknowledge their great values and the pivotal roles they play in cultivating our future leaders.

We must equip our teachers and schools with the resources they need to make the average class size ten students or less. We must help them develop systems that effectively measure where our kids need help and reward the systems that produce outcomes that can be measured by how our kids perform against their peers in other countries.

I played a game as a child—although I was not very good at it—called "Follow the Leader." I was not good at this game because I had a hard time following behind a person I did not deem to be a leader. When I think about our kids and our current educational system, I wonder, what are we preparing them to be? Robots with the ability to regurgitate the answers needed to take a standardized test? Hamsters that are required to enroll in so many advanced classes and burn out in college because they are so exhausted from high school? Drifters with no imagination who need some type of stimulus to activate independent thinking? I already stated this, but our current education system is not working, and we must act now. I genuinely hope we can change the current trajectory of our educational roadmap by putting each kid on a course that will get them excited about learning, invigorated by knowledge that will arm them with tools required to solve the world's most complex problems. I would settle for being in the top twenty in the world in science, reading, and mathematics. I also will settle for kids of color, especially Black boys, getting the longer end of the stick by having access to programs inside and outside of school to help them build a strong foundation for their education.

COVID-19 robbed us of so much in 2020, but it has allowed us to reimagine how our kids are educated. Let's not waste this time bickering about sending our kids back to a woefully unprepared building to keep them safe. Yes, I understand instructing kids at home, maintaining a job, and managing a household is certainly not something any of us would have signed up for in 2020. Now that we are here, let's work together to get through this rough time, but, in parallel, imagine the education we wish we had, where all students are provided with what they need regardless of where they live, what they look like, and how they learn. Whatever you imagine our school system to be, please remember it must include all kids instead of only yours.

SHARING AND RACISM:
DO AS I SAY AND NOT AS I DO

I t was not long ago I had school-aged kids. One of their pastimes was playing in a sandbox. Okay, to be fully transparent, the sandbox was a shotput pit at a local middle school we frequented to get in a quick run around the track. My three kids had mixed emotions about going to the middle school track because they knew I would require them to run a lap or two before they could play in the shotput pit.

On one such occasion, as I was running around the track, I noticed a few kids had joined mine in the shotput pit. One of the kids had a bright yellow bucket, and another had a few tools such as a shovel, rake, and star-shaped mold. When I approached the pit, I noticed the kids were playing together, sharing their tools, and having a good time. The parents of the kids who joined mine were watching from the bleacher and conversing with one another. After I completed my last lap, I told my kids it was time to go, and they waved good-bye to their new acquaintances. Other than a variety of skin colors (black/brown/white) represented in the pit, the kids were typical kids wanting to play and have a good time.

I reflect upon this time because I wonder how is it that as kids, we can get it right and share, and somehow, between adolescence and adulthood, we become selfish and want to keep everything to ourselves or share with only a select few? In many instances, kids are taught to share and play nicely with each other by their parents. The question I ponder is, is there a correlation between sharing and racism?

Let's explore this question by first finding a cogent definition for sharing. Businessdictionary.com defines a share as "a unit of ownership that represents an equal proportion of a company's capital."[5] It entitles its holders (the shareholders) to an equal claim on the company's profits and equal obligation for the company's debts and losses. I'm sure I have now lost a few of you because you are wondering why I would use a definition in the context of ownership in the world.

The genesis of slavery stems from white men forcing Black people to perform work against their own will to generate income and, in many instances, wealth. There was no sharing going on because Black people were considered subhuman and were defined by the contributions they made to pad their oppressors' pockets.

The ownership question surfaces because society reminds people of color that we were brought to North America on slave ships, and we did not own anything nor were entitled to anything. It does not matter that Black people were enslaved for centuries to build the United States into the center of prosperity it is today; they were repaid by creating systems of oppression that were virtually impossible for most to escape. Even in death, the cycle of oppression reverberated through their descendants.

What I appreciate about kids and sharing is the reciprocation aspect. You share, I share. On the other hand, adults share, but often it is transactional, requiring something in return, which sullies the intent of sharing. Racism exists in the United States and beyond because the dominant population, white people, do not want to share. I wish sharing were confined to money. But it goes far deeper.

For instance, several US billionaires have chosen to give their wealth away to support causes to improve the quality of life for all human beings. On the surface, their act of benevolence is quite noble, but the challenge is the philanthropic organizations these donations will filter to are generally not headed by people of color. Let's be clear—who and what these billionaires give their money to is their prerogative. The opportunity is for these same billionaires to make a bold statement and require the organizations they offer their wealth to be run by the very people it helps. It also would be life-changing for these same people to create companies designed to eradicate racism as well as to hire people of color in leadership positions within their current companies. Donating money to civic organizations is great, but none of these organizations have the power and influence as these billionaires do. I suppose we should be presenting this idea to legislatures, but as we have experienced, they are only willing to kick the can down the street.

Undoubtedly, the sharing problem is not limited to the wealthy. What about a person of color who graduates from college with honors but has no advocate to speak on their behalf? Where do you suppose they end up working their first job out of college? The answer: places that do not require a college degree and/or high school diploma. These same young people are probably saddled with student loans and no real resolution to turn their situation around. In the meantime, their white contemporaries generally have an advocate who can help them get their foot in the door and do not have to work a job that does not align with their academic credentials or professional capabilities. A more equitable approach would be to create programs to guarantee people of color opportunities upon their completion of a four-year degree. Whose responsibility is it to make this happen? It is all our responsibility—especially the CEOs and leaders of the companies that make up our private and public sectors.

It has been said that "Children are the greatest imitators. So give them something great to imitate." Before adults' selfishness and entitlement taint kids, they share with and have no problem reaching out to their fellow playmates, regardless of their skin color.

To build a better America, we must share. Sharing is supposed to make you feel good, but for some reason, sharing in America is associated with socialism, weakness, power, and many other social dichotomies that impede our progress. We must bring the shotput pit to the consciousness of America and start intentionally sharing with people who do not look like us. Sharing is the fuel that can ignite the engine of prosperity and should not be relegated exclusively to our kids to dispense.

POWER TO THE BLACK WOMEN

W omen are the vines that enable life as we know it to exist. I cannot think of anything on this earth that did not have a woman's hand involved in its maturation. Nevertheless, society tends to measure women by their beauty and body types versus their intellectual prowess and intuitive ability to evoke change, with violence serving as a last resort rather than the first. Shirley Chisholm asserted, "Tremendous amounts of talent are being lost to our society just because that talent wears a skirt." While skirts are certainly no longer required, Chisholm was right that the power of women is often overlooked—and perhaps feminine power is what is needed for social change.

I have the great fortune to have many great women in my life—my mother, grandmothers, sisters, spouse, daughter, relatives, friends, and colleagues. These women come in a variety of skin colors, but it is the Black women who have made indelible contributions in my life, and for that, I say, "Power to Black women."

What makes Black women so great? Is it their enduring spirit and unwavering support when others have turned their backs on them? Is it their willingness to correct you when you are wrong and push you to do better, challenging the pronouncement of the majority? Is it their commitment to excellence even when others attempt to silence them? Is it their ability to hide the pain of being a Black woman by braving life with a strong fist and shedding their silent tears in the confines of their bedroom? The question may be rhetorical, but the answers are complex and can be found in typical Black women's actions.

My mother, Frances L. Reaves, is the epitome of a great Black woman. What makes her so great? I believe it was the marathon mentality she followed by raising four out of five kids after my father's passing, without outside financial assistance or wine breaks from friends or family members, never complaining about what she did not have or her circumstances. She worked the graveyard shift (11:00 p.m. to 7:00 a.m.) that started at 9:00 p.m.

because she had to walk a half of a mile to a bus stop in the blistering cold and sweltering summers to catch two buses to work.

I sometimes think my mom was on some artificial version of adrenaline because she watched my older sisters and cousin's kids throughout the day when she should have been resting. In other words, she received approximately five hours of sleep a day and worked nearly nineteen hours in some capacity for over twenty years. My mom is retired now, but what she did to provide for her family is what many Black women in our past and present continue to do today. For in many instances, the only support they have is their creativity to make a better world for their children and other family members they tend to be responsible for taking care of.

Black women are a sparkling twenty-carat yellow diamond that is often overlooked by our world. I believe they must be praised for being the wheels on the car that continues to run even when the gas tank is on empty and no gas station is in sight. I cannot imagine what this world would be like without Black women, but I sure know we all must do a better job of honoring them because so many of us would not be who we are without Black women.

MY FIRST CONFRONTATION WITH A POLICE OFFICER: THREE DECADES LATER, I CANNOT FORGET IT

E very year, my grade-school principal invited police officers to our school to chat with us about the importance of getting good grades, listening to our teachers, and staying away from trouble. The program was called "Officer Friendly" and was designed to expose kids to police officers and promote positive relations between the kids and their communities. This was the only time that I saw a police officer smile and shake hands with anyone. Regrettably, police officers frequented my childhood neighborhood only in response to a shooting or while carrying out a drug bust. These images of police officers are what I would remember, and at an early age, I surmised that it was best that I stayed the hell away from them. For most of my teenage and early adult years, I was quite fortunate to have no interaction with the police—until I bought my first car.

As a black man living in the nation's capital in the late eighties/early nineties, Washington, DC, held the ominous title of the "Murder Capital of the World." Everywhere you looked, somebody was being carried off in a body bag or in chains and shackles. When I decided to return to Washington, DC, after college, I thought as long as I stayed out of the way of drug dealers and the police, I would be fine. I managed to avoid the wrath of drug dealers—but not the police.

My first incident with the police feels like it was yesterday, although it was August 24, 1989. I was driving along the parkway when I heard a siren. I first ignored it, but as the sirens got louder and closer, the police officers announced on his loud-speaker to pull over, and I promptly stopped on the median. He proceeded to approach the car and told me to get out and put my hands up. In shock, I did what the officer said and got out of my car and put my hands on my head. I asked, "What did I do?"

He responded, "Is this your car?"

I said yes and asked him if he would like to see my registration and license. He said no and indicated my car must be stolen because I was too young to drive such a nice car. He then told me to put my hands on my car so he could pat me down. I kept asking the officers what I did to deserve this treatment. He told me to shut up before he hit me with his baton. Oddly, as he was frisking me, there was a metro bus thirty feet away from my car at a traffic light. Several people on the bus were hanging out of the window, yelling at the cop, "Leave him alone." As I heard the people shouting, one of the people called out my name. To this day, I have no idea who that person was, but they may have saved my life because the officers stopped frisking me and told me to get in my car and not to look back. When I arrived back in my neighborhood, I saw a few local guys gathered on the corner, and I shared my experience with them about the police. Their counsel to me was, "You are lucky you were not shot." This experience left me forever traumatized by the police, and every time I see a police car behind my car at a traffic light, my mind flashes to the August 24, 1989, incident.

For several years, when I was driving my car, I continued to be harassed by police officers—yes, white men who wore a badge and seemed to stop me at least twice a month. Their routine was to follow me for a few moments to see how I would respond and then drive away after a few moments.

On October 13, 1995, I had my second incident with a police officer that required me to get out of my car. I was driving along a parkway in Virginia with my spouse and unborn child. Like August 24, 1989, the police officer asked me to get out of my car for no reason. He asked me for my license and registration, and once I gave it to him, I asked him, "What did I do? Why did you stop me?"

He did not respond and began to walk around my car. As he walked around the car, my spouse asked him the same question, "What did he do? Why did you stop us?" He had no real explanation and eventually gave me back my license and registration, and we went on our way. I had not had any other interactions of this nature with a police officer since this incident and will never shake these images for as long as I live.

When I think about all of the Black men and women who lost their lives at the hands of police officers, I do not have any real answers as to why my life was spared and why their lives were not. I do not understand why the immediate remedy to quell an altercation between some police officers and a Black man ends with the Black man in a body bag. How is it that a white man on August 3, 2019, sprayed an El Paso, Texas Walmart with bullets, killed twenty-two people, wounded twenty-six others, and was apprehended with only handcuffs?

What about the white man who killed eleven parishioners and wounded six on November 17, 2018, at the Tree of Life Synagogue in Pittsburgh, Pennsylvania? Why didn't officers subdue *him* with their knees to his neck?

How about the massacre on June 17, 2015, in Charleston, South Carolina, where the congregation prayed for their assailant, and he showed his appreciation by killing nine of them and wounding one? Why in the world was this assailant treated to Burger King by the police?

What about on August 4, 2020, in Aurora, Colorado, when a sea of police officers emptied a Black family from their van, handcuffed most of them, and placed them on the ground because they received word the van was stolen? How did the police get their facts so wrong when the item that was stolen was a motorcycle with the same license number but from another state? Why did this Black family deserve to get this treatment? How would the same situation have been handled if this family was white? A van, or in this instance, a motorcycle, can be replaced, but the mental anguish this family, especially the children, will not be healed with just an apology.

How about a protest on August 25, 2020, in Kenosha, Wisconsin calling to end police brutality ending in two innocent, unarmed persons being sprayed with bullets and several people being injured? Several eyewitnesses identified the gunman to the police officers. Their pleas were ignored. Oddly, the gunman carrying an automatic assault rifle put his hand up, but the police did not stop him and ask him any questions, like why are you carrying an assault rifle? Perhaps they did not ask him any questions because of his white skin color. How many Black men can walk down a US street with an assault rifle without being stopped or potentially killed by the police?

It does not matter if the Black man or anyone of color is committing a crime or abiding by the law—no encounter with police officers should ever end like Laquan McDonald's, being shot sixteen times on October 20, 2014, because he was walking away from the police.

Or like Freddie Gray, who was being arrested for possession of a switchblade on April 12, 2015, and fifteen minutes later, found dead in a police wagon with a severed spinal cord, handcuffed, and feet shackled.

Or, like Sandra Bland, found hanging from a sheet in a jail cell after being arrested for being argumentative with a police officer on July 13, 2015.

Or like Alton Sterling for selling CDs and DVDs outside of a shop. He was tased, pinned to the ground, and then shot six times by police on July 5, 2016.

Or, like Philando Castille, pulled over in a traffic stop on July 6, 2016, and was killed in front of his family after he told them he had a legal firearm in the glove compartment of his car.

Or, like Botham Jean, on September 6, 2018, sitting on his sofa in his apartment, eating ice cream and was killed because the off-duty police officer mistakenly thought he was in her apartment.

Or, like Jacob Blake, on August 23, 2020, walking away from police officers only to be shot seven times in the back while his three young sons watched. Jacob Blake survived his shooting but will likely suffer permanent paralysis from the waist down.

These events are reminiscent of how slave owners beat Blacks into submission or killed them when they felt they had no more use for their services. It is the police's job to serve and protect the people, but I wonder when people of color, especially Black men, will no longer be subjected to slave-like tactics when encountering the police. What do we have to do? Ask for burgers and fries?

COLORISM AND PEOPLE OF COLOR: THE CONVERSATION MUST START AT HOME

B lack, brown, caramel, light-skinned, dark-skinned, red, others—all possess positive and negative connotations in the eye of the beholder. But for many white people, they see these shades as only black or brown. As a person of color, I never understood the purpose of calling someone anything outside of their birth name, but that is another essay for another time.

Colorism generally occurs when persons of the same ethnicity discriminate against persons who are darker-skinned. The lighter-skinned persons within that ethnicity are deemed to be better-looking and worthy of more reverence than their dark-skinned counterparts. The conversation about colorism tends to be dominated by African-Americans, but Latinos and Asians also struggle with colorism within their ethnicity.

Society does not have a problem with promoting these horrible phenomena in the movies that we see (white is best, but lighter is okay), on the magazine covers that we follow (whiteness dominates the pages read by light-skinned people), as well as how we will be treated by the criminal justice system based on the shade of our skin.

Dr. Monk, a Harvard sociologist, penned a 2018 study in the *Ethnic and Racial Studies* journal indicating the probability of being arrested and how long someone goes to jail is based their skin shade, with darker-skinned Black persons being likely to be arrested, and if they receive jail time, it will be much longer than their lighter-skinned Black peers. [6]Racism, which is discrimination against a person because of his or her race, is already a quandary that appears to have no end. In contrast, colorism adds an additional layer that makes it almost impossible to eliminate racial and skin-shade discrimination.

My first experience with colorism happened before I could even open my eyes and recognize my parents. I was born to wonderful parents who happened to be dark-skinned African Americans, and I was, well, much lighter than my parents and had green eyes. It did not help the nurse at the hospital where I was born initially refused to allow my parents to take me home because I did not look like my parents. While I do not recall my parents making a big fuss of my different skin tone from theirs and my five other siblings, my siblings had no problem with calling me everything except my name. In fact, the ongoing joke in my immediate family was that I was adopted, and my parents had mercy on me and gave me a home.

While these mean-spirited comments from my sisters and brothers hurt, I learned the art of quick wit, deflected these comments, and intentionally demeaned my siblings. I did learn over time the power of words and refrained from verbally attacking my siblings even when they nearly would bring me to tears. The jokes about how different I looked from my family were not limited to my siblings. Whether I was outside playing with kids in the neighborhood or posing for a family picture, there was always some question about why I was much lighter-skinned than my family members.

What I have grown to understand about colorism is it does not matter what shade your skin color may be, discrimination feels the same and everyone's feelings should be respected when this topic is discussed. It is easy to see why darker-skinned Blacks feel their plight with race is much harder than a Black person with lighter skin, but the reality is that we are all in this together, and we must stop throwing one another under the bus when colorism is discussed.

The conversation about colorism must start at home. My siblings made jokes about colorism, but we never talked about it. I suspect we did not know how. If we had been able to have this conversation, I would want to better understand why they felt they had to make fun of my skin shade, and if they were aware of how it made me feel. I also would like to know how they felt about their skin shade and what obstacles do they believe they have experienced because of their darker skin?

I recently had a conversation with a friend who is a dark-skinned Black man, and he confirmed the perception that lighter-skinned Black men do not have as many challenges as darker-skinned Black men. I had to remind him that on occasion, I still hear triple clicks from alarm chirps when I pass by a car driven by a white person and notice white women clutching their purses when on the same elevator ride. Our experiences may feel different because of our interpretation. Still, in the end, these are the same discriminatory behaviors that cannot be tolerated, and they are not reserved for only darker-skinned Black people.

Racial discrimination may not be an action that people of color can influence. Still, colorism is a problem that can be significantly minimized if we first acknowledge it is a problem within our ethnicities. Matshona Dhliwayo, a Canadian philosopher, said, "Wisdom from a stranger is better than ignorance from a friend." We do not have to wait for someone else from another ethnicity or outside of our family or circle of friends to tell us how to correct something that is in our capacity to solve. The question then becomes: Do we want to?

THE SPIRIT OF LIVING
AS A BLACK MAN IN AMERICA

I gets weary
Sick of trying
I'm tired of living
Feared of dying
But ol' man river
He's rolling along

The above lyrics were written by Jerome Kerr and Oscar Hammerstein II for a musical, *Showboat*, which premiered on Broadway on December 27, 1927. The show was about the lives of the performers, stagehands, and dock workers on the *Cotton Blossom*, a Mississippi River showboat from 1887 to 1927. Two white men may have written

his song, but it is Paul Robeson, an American actor and political activist, who played the role of Joe on Broadway and brought the anguish and hopelessness of this character to life. His delivery of the song "Ole Man River" was so mesmerizing that few, if any, others who played this role were able to emulate it. I had the enjoyable experience of playing the role of Joe in my college rendition of *Showboat*, and little did I know that years later, I would still reflect on a song that has more meaning to me today than it did when I sang it over three decades ago.

When I was in the second grade, my teacher asked everyone what they would like to be when they grow up. Many of the students said doctors, lawyers, firefighters, or teachers, and I said to the teacher I would like to be alive to see my next birthday. My teacher was stunned, but she did not ask me to clarify. She just told me to go read a book at the library station in our classroom. To provide some perspective of what was going on around me during this time in my life, soldiers were coming home from Vietnam, my great-grandmother on my father's side had recently died, and three days before her death, a man laid outside of my apartment door face down with a bullet in his head after an altercation with a drug dealer. The only thing I could think about was surviving the here and now, not my future.

I think about the millions of kids around the world who have suffered violent deaths from wars, human trafficking, genocide, and many other horrible untimely means. I have no idea what it is like to be in these types of circumstances, but it is my belief that regardless of how horrible or inhuman an event may be, that does not discount what someone else has experienced in their life that may have caused physical and psychological trauma.

Fast forward a few years—I was in middle school, and I was on the steps of my apartment building, watching a few of the neighborhood kids jumping rope and playing tag. Sitting across from me were a few young men who were romanticizing about how they planned to play football in college, and that was the first time that I seriously thought about college. My oldest sister was a schoolteacher, but she did not talk about her college experience.

I asked one of the guys how I could apply to college, and another chimed in and said: "Why are you asking? You will never finish high school." While I did not understand why he made this statement to me, I shrugged it off and never got the answer, at least at that moment, about applying to college. Little did this guy know that I would go on to complete high school, college, and graduate school. It is easy to see how hopelessness can invade people of color's psyche with little effort.

People of color are told at an early age by our families and society that we have to be twice as good as many of our white counterparts at whatever we do to get ahead. This means we must be better in school, sports, thinking, and life. This bar is frankly outrageous, and while everyone should make the best effort, people of color sometimes feel the high bar is so far out of reach that many of us can empathize with the above lyrics of, "Sick of trying, tired of living but fear dying." This can be especially burdensome for Black men because of society's deep attitudes that constantly remind us that we are good enough to play on a football field but not smart enough to own the field.

Black men have been defined way too long by our physical stature and bravado and not our minds. I suppose that working on plantation fields, fighting wars, and being forced to work on chain gangs does not help our image, but we are so much more than our appearance.

Some Black men elevate this façade by calling men who do not play sports "weak" and thinking that reading a book and getting an education is somehow reserved for Black women and white people. When I think about our ancestors and the thousands of people who died because they were trying to learn to read, I realize this mode of thinking must be eliminated from the conscious of any Black man that holds on to the awful fallacy. Society can help improve how some Black men view ourselves by encouraging us to apply the same rigor we put into dribbling a basketball into reading about basketball. It is a reality that Black men who play professional sports generate wealth for themselves and many others who are around them. I would surmise if more effort is placed on generating opportunities for Black men, the amount of individual wealth would be less, but the systemic wealth that would transcend Black men's lives, and thus society, would be far greater and impactful inside and outside of the communities in which Black men reside.

Other Black men have the perception that because they have somehow been accepted by a small circle of white society, that any other Black man can pull themselves out of poverty and despair with hard work. I wish this recipe for success was true, but for most Black men, their skin color will generally determine how they are defined by our society, regardless of what they have accomplished. The test? Just watch a Black man walk down any street in America, in a predominantly white neighborhood or city. Perhaps if the Black man is a celebrity, someone may recognize him, but he still will be seen as a Black man.

Black men come in a variety of sizes, skin shades, and talents, and we want to give to a world that spends more time telling us what we are not and what they want us to be. We are sons who are tired of our mothers standing over our caskets because our lives were snuffed out because of circumstances outside of our control. We are fathers and uncles to children who are taught by society not to have confidence in us because we are violent and will only end up in jail or dead. We are survivors who continue to find ways to live in a world that wants us to shut up and give up by denying us access to options that would make our lives better and the world a better place for everyone.

Regardless of our circumstances, no matter how long the road may seem, Black men are resilient, and even amid our darkest moments, as the song above states, "But ole' man river, he just keeps rolling along." As a Black man, I do not just want to keep rolling along; I want to fly.

Dick Gregory, an accomplished comedian and civil rights activist, titled his autobiography *Called the N-word*. It chronologized his life in America and his struggle to be seen as more than just a Black man. This book was written a half a century ago, but a number of his struggles are what many Black men, myself included, still experience fifty years later. My question is, will I always be a ▓▓▓▓ in America?

ABOUT THE AUTHOR

John A. Reaves, a Washington, DC native has lived and worked in 8 states and has been employed with several Fortune 100 Multinational companies. He is married and has three adult children, and resides in Matthews, NC, a suburb of Charlotte. John possesses a BS in Speech Communication from Radford, University, MAIS in Organizational Communication from George Mason University, and a PhD in Information Systems Management from Walden University. John is an avid runner and writer.

ENDNOTES

1   America's Founding Documents. (2020). Retrieved August 28, 2020, from https://www.archives.gov/

2   DeSilver, D. (2017, February 15). U.S. academic achievement lags that of many other countries. Retrieved August 28, 2020, from https://www.pew research.org/fact-tank/2017/02/15/u-s-students-inter nationally-math-science/

3   What Type Of Learner Is Your Child? (2019, May 28). Retrieved August 28, 2020, from https://gradepower learning.com/what-type-learner-is-my-child/

4   Ferguson, D., Valk, A., Collins, C., & Pleepow. (2019, Fall). Black Minds Matter. Retrieved August 28, 2020, from https://www.tolerance.org/magazine/fall-2019/black-minds-matter

5   Online Business Dictionary - BusinessDictionary.com. (n.d.). Retrieved August 28, 2020, from http://www. businessdictionary.com/

6   Ellis P. Monk (2019) The color of punishment: African Americans, skin tone, and the criminal justice system, Ethnic and Racial Studies, 42:10, 1593-1612, DOI: 10.1080/01419870.2018.1508736